MARY'S STORY
the rescue, the life

BY
Lucia Baldinelli Ciampa

My Mom's nickname was Mary and that's where
Mary got her name!

A little piece of heaven
from above.

It was a beautiful day.   I went for a stroll in our Country Land. We were new to the world so we wanted to see everything!

My brother and I wandered off by ourselves, away from the rest of the family. Before we knew it, we were lost! All we saw were wooded bushy areas. We had a hard time walking through the branches. Suddenly, my foot got stuck in the branches and I couldn't get out. We're in big trouble now we thought! My brother couldn't get me out so he left to go find our Mom.

I was alone and stuck in the prickly branches. I cried and cried until I fell fast asleep.

I woke up shaking my head, remembering where I was.   I heard splashing nearby.
"Quack, quack!" said the duck.   "Hello, hello!" I yelled out but
nobody heard me.   The ducks swam away.   I'm doomed I thought to myself.
I should never have left to go out on my own.

I wondered if anyone was ever going to find me.

"Hello little one, don't worry" said the Monarch butterfly. "I will stay right here and watch over you."

Soon it would be dark. I was hungry and tired. "Wait, I hear voices coming from over there!" I cried, trying to squiggle my head towards the voices. A boy and a girl were talking and moving towards a park bench. They kept talking to each other and looking my way. Did they see me? Could they hear me crying? I can hear them!

It felt like a lot of time went by. Out of nowhere the boy and the girl picked me up from the bush and put me in a warm blanket. I was saved! Good bye butterfly! Thank you for watching over me!

I just arrived at my new home!   I'm so thirsty and hungry but I am safe!

My new Mom is a human Mom. She makes kissing noises, cuddles with me, bathes me, cleans my poops and sings to me. It's pretty cool that she named me after her Mom. Her Moms name was Mary. Her Mom had just passed away eight months ago. Taking care of me let her feel less sad.   I felt less sad too.

I was kind of a bad girl today. Mom brought me outside today and put me on the grass. I started running across the street. Boy was my Mom mad! The faster I ran, the faster she ran. I thought it was quite funny but she didn't. This was the first time I heard my Mom scream at me. She chased me around until she caught me!

Now I know what it means when someone says you're on time-out or you're grounded!

Here I am in my new bright pink swimming pool. This is way better than being in a box! There is so much room here! Mom feeds me grass and bird seed. So yummy! She also keeps a bowl of water near me too.

Mom says I'm a Canada Goose! Baby geese which are called goslings, take about a month to hatch. Babies are covered with soft feathers called down. We hatch with our eyes open and leave the nest within 24 hours, following our parents. Goslings can swim right away. In less than two months, the goslings grow adult feathers and learn to fly.

I am so proud to be a Canada Goose. Mom bought me a surf board with the Red Maple Leaf. I love it!

Yes, this is me dangling upside down. I am showing off my swimming skills of course! Can you swim like this? If you can't then I would love to show you how.

Did you know that goslings can dive and swim for 30-40 feet under water?

I'm getting faster and faster! Want to come swimming with me?

I'm so lucky that my Mom lets me swim in the grown-up pool! My Mom, my new sister and new brother are swimming with me too!

This is what I look like after I go swimming. I look like a soft little fluff ball. You're probably wondering why my Mom lets me go swimming in the big pool. She said I can swim in the big pool because I am little and it's easy for her to clean up all my poops! I guess I better enjoy it while I can!

Time to soak up some Sun. So much fun!

Say hello to my Aunt Mila! She is a Boxer puppy.

Aunt Mila loved me the moment she saw me! She was fascinated with me.

Everywhere I went, Aunt Mila wanted to go too. Mom wouldn't let her though because she was much bigger than me. I was really scared of her at first. She looked like a giant monster!

Mom actually put her in the water the same time as me but Aunt Mila would swim straight to the step. She wasn't as good of a swimmer as me. Aunt Mila had to be taught how to swim. I instantly knew how to swim because I am a goose. That's okay, we are both good at different things.

Mom is teaching me how to get out of the pool. One step …
two steps … and out I go. Not bad for a two-month old baby goose!

Silly me! I forgot to tell you that my birthday is on April 25th, 2020.
Mom says that I have the same birthday as her Nana Elena. How special is that?!?!

Me with Aunt Mila.

Pee-a-boo! Here I am! Hi Aunt Mila! Would you like me to share some of my organic lettuce with you?

Time is flying by! I'm not so little anymore!

Well hello stranger! I bet you didn't recognize me! It's me Mary.
I'm about nine weeks old now and growing so fast.

My feathers are darker and my little wings are getting much bigger. My
head and my neck are still baby yellow.

My Mom took this picture of me after I ate, so don't mind the
food on my beak. Can you guess what I was eating?

Shhhh….   Don't tell my Mom that I'm trying to find a
way to get my food. One jump, two jumps, three… Nope.
There is no way I'm going to be able to reach. Do you think you
can help me?

If I only had a ladder.

My Mom took this pretty neat picture of me. Do you like it? She loves taking pictures of me and sometimes a little too much!

I'm getting bigger, taller and my neck is getting longer. If you look closely, you can see my baby blue wing tips.

My Mom doesn't put me in the pool as much anymore because I poop a lot more now. I'm only allowed a quick dip and playtime and then I go inside to take a bath. My Mom likes to hold me in a blanket at night until I fall asleep.

Beach time! Family time! My very first time at the beach! Yay!! This is one of our Beach Houses. My older sister Susannah and my older brother Joey are playing bean bag toss. I'm just walking around, checking everything out. It's so exciting! A little later, Mom and Dad brought me, my doggy sister Jasmine, doggy brother Duke and doggy Aunt Mila for a walk.

Do you know who this is in the picture? Yes! That's right, it's me Mary!
I'm a big girl now! Five months old.

About me:

The Canada Goose has a long black neck and head with a white band on its cheeks that
runs under the chin like a strap. We have black feet and a light tan body with lighter
brown or white under our tails.   Our black bill has comb-like ridges on the sides,
or teeth, around the outside edges that are used as a cutting tool. Males and females
look alike, although females are usually a little smaller than the males. I am a female.
My wings have grown so big and I am learning to fly!

It's so beautiful and relaxing out here. This is where our other beach house is. There is so much grass everywhere which means so much more for me to eat! Mom says she's going to call this Mary's Island after me. I kind of feel like a Princess! Now I will just need to find my Prince.

This is a picture of a Hawk. Mom had to keep an eye on me when I was smaller because of the Hawks. They would circle around looking for their next prey. I wouldn't take any chances to hang around one of those for sure!

The picture above says, "Spread Your Wings and Fly" in Italian. My Mom comes from an Italian background. I think that's pretty cool.

Bath time! I have my own private bathtub!   After hours of playing outside in the dirt, Mom gets my bath ready. I love bath time. I swim and play in the water and Mom gives me snacks in the water.

Sometimes I'm a bad girl and I jump out of the tub and poop on the floor. Mom gets pretty mad when I do that, so I try not to do it very much. It sure is fun though!

I have my own bedroom and my own bathtub. I am a Princess after all!

Wow! What is all this white stuff!? So cool! My first snowfall. Lots of snow everywhere! I love it! It's so cold and fluffy. I can jump up and down in it. I can eat it too! Here we come swan dive!

I can't even see my feet!

More than one goose is called geese. Here are some interesting information about birds that live outside.

Many ducks, geese, pelicans, gulls and swans keep body heat by standing on one leg or even sitting down. Geese tuck their feet and beaks into their rich downy feathers which keep them warm and also helps them breathe warmer air.

I don't have to worry about the freezing cold because my Mom doesn't keep me out for long when it's super cold and I stay in the house overnight. Geese protect themselves by sleeping in water overnight to keep away from predators. Geese do not have good night vision.

Most geese fly South for the winter but there are a lot that stay where they are.

It's such a beautiful winter day. The sun is big, beautiful and warm.
Time for a winter wonderland swim!

That was so much fun! Time to get out. I'm going to spread my wings and fly!

Did you know that when we pluck our feathers they grow back?

Looks like it's going to snow again. What's your favorite time of the year?

Mom decided it was time for a winter road trip to the beach. There were lots of geese, ducks and a couple of swans too! Mom wants me to play with them but I'm not ready to make new friends quite yet. I just want to explore on my own for now.

This is the first time I actually went into the water at the beach. In the summer time the waves were really high and scary and I was much younger then too. I'm bigger, stronger and have more courage now! The water was very cold but my feathers keep me warm, except for my feet!

Two hours went by. It was getting late and Mom was freezing. Time to go home. It was fun at the lake in the winter time too! Can't wait to go back soon.

Home again! Mom said it's time for a bath.

Mom bought me this little duck for my bath. I did not like her at first! I didn't want to share my bath time with anyone!

After my bath time comes bedtime. Good night everyone!

Sweet dreams!

I'm only nine months old right now. When I turn three years old, I will be able to mate and have my own goslings which are baby geese. When geese lay eggs, they take between 28-35 days to hatch.

I can't wait to have a family of my own one day!

Aunt Mila is that you?

Surprise!!! My Aunt Mila just had puppies!! They are so cute. I love them all. Can you guess how many puppies there are?

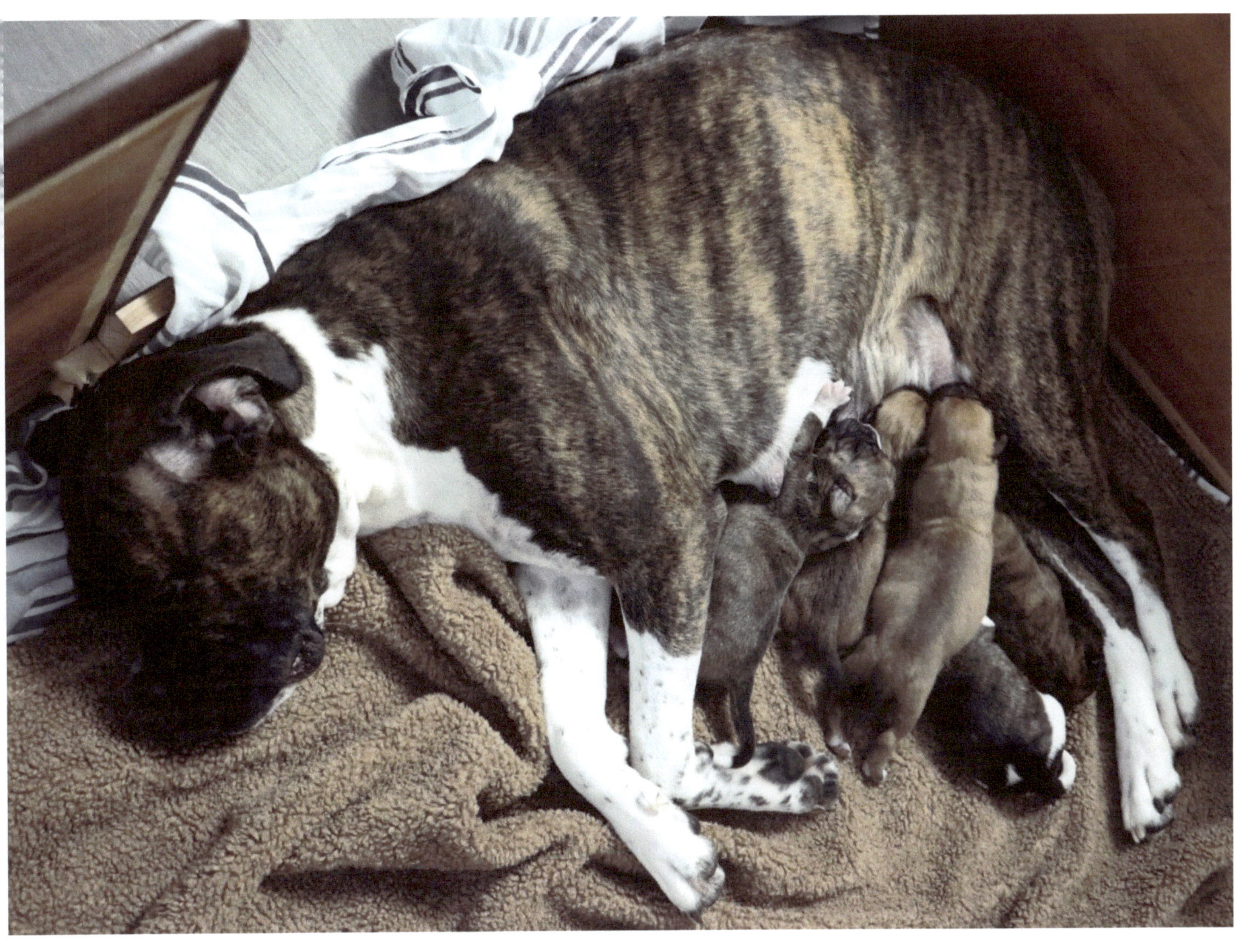

There are five puppies! It looks like it's feeding time!
Congratulations Aunt Mila. Xo

What a beautiful little family you have there!

"SPREAD YOUR WINGS AND FLY"

BASED ON A TRUE STORY

Time to go!   I hope you enjoyed the story of my life. I enjoyed sharing it with you! Remember:

BELIEVE IN YOU
I do!

LOVE

Do you like my baby picture?

@wishes2312